PLANET IN CRISIS
POLLUTION
CRISIS

This edition published in 2009 by:
The Rosen Publishing Group, Inc.
29 East 21st Street
New York, NY 10010

Copyright © 2009 David West Books

Designed and produced by
David West Books

Editor: James Pickering
Picture Research: Carlotta Cooper

Photo Credits: Abbreviations: t-top, m-middle, b-bottom, r-right,
l-left, c-center.

Front cover tl & 5r BNFL/Sellafield; b - Rex Features Ltd. Pages: 3 (Edward Parker); 7r, 11tr (Julio Etchart);
8br, 14–15b, 24bl, 30 (Mark Edwards); 9bl, 21m (Martin Bond); 10–11 (Al Pavangkanan); 10br (Chris
Brown); 11ml (Bruce Durling); 13tr (Thomas Raupach); 14m, 20bl (Ray Pfortner); 15bl & r (Adrian Arbib);
17tr (Hartmut Schwarzbach); 17br (Kevin Schafer); 17m (U.S. Coastguard); 17bl (Sara Atkins); 21t
(Christopher & Amy Cate Esposito); 21br (Peter Van den Bossche); 24–25 (John Maier); 25m (Herbert
Giradet); 27m (Dave Watts); 27b (Nick Cobbing) - Still Pictures. 4tr, 4–5, 7tl & bl, 9br, 10bl, 13bl, 16tr,
16–17, 19bl & br, 26t, 27t, 28t, 29t - Rex Features Ltd. 25b (Michael Pereckas); 6tr, 12bl & br, 14bl, 22l &
r, 23t - Corbis Images. 22–23 - © Greenpeace/Steve Morgan. 23b - Courtesy of Babcock Hitachi. 29b -
Minamata City, Kumamoto, Japan.

Library of Congress Cataloging-in-Publication Data

Parker, Russ, 1970-
 Pollution crisis / Russ Parker.
   p. cm. -- (Planet in crisis)
 Includes bibliographical references and index.
 ISBN 978-1-4358-5252-5 (library binding) -- ISBN 978-1-4358-0682-5 (pbk.) -- ISBN 978-1-4358-0688-7
 (6-pack)
 1. Pollution--Juvenile literature. I. Title.
 TD176.P37 2009
 363.73--dc22

                              2008043749

Printed and bound in China

First published in Great Britain by Heinemann Library, a division of Reed Educational and Professional Publishing Limited.

PLANET IN CRISIS

POLLUTION CRISIS

Russ Parker

rosen publishing's
rosen
central

New York

CONTENTS

Restless oceans spread pollution around the globe, carrying trash and chemicals thousands of miles to remote shores.

Today's industries give us endless products, machines, gadgets, and comforts, but at the cost of turning landscapes into polluted wastelands.

INTRODUCTION

Almost everywhere in our world, there is pollution. Yet we often don't see it. Some forms of pollution are invisible, such as rain water that contains acids or toxic chemicals seeping into the ground. Other types of pollution are so familiar that we hardly notice, like fumes from cars or a local river empty of life. Few places on Earth are pollution-free. But with time and effort, the world is gradually being made cleaner and safer from this modern menace.

Nuclear power stations make huge amounts of radioactive wastes, yet no one knows how to dispose of them safely.

Pollution is anything that causes harm, trouble, or problems in our surroundings, or environment. It is also part of modern living. As we eat, learn, work, travel, and enjoy ourselves, we either make pollution or contribute to it.

POLLUTION BY SUBSTANCES

Some pollution is in the form of substances and chemicals. These might be liquids, gases, or objects made from metals, plastics, and similar materials. Pollution occurs when these substances collect where they should not be.

Electricity is our most convenient form of energy. But making and distributing it causes immense amounts of pollution.

THE WORLD GLOWS BRIGHTER

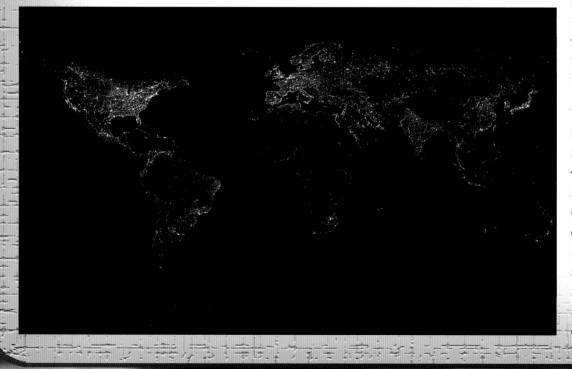

Every year the world glows brighter. Seen here in 2007, lights from street lamps, buildings, advertising, vehicles, and sports stadiums fill the night sky with a bright glow —especially in built-up regions. This form of energy pollution causes many problems. Some people cannot sleep, bats and owls are almost blinded, and astronomers cannot see the stars.

Hot topic
During the 2000s, a new pollution problem developed over South and Southeast Asia. The "Asian brown cloud" is a mix of fire, smoke, and fumes from vehicles, factories, and power stations. It spreads as far as Australia.

The brown haze stays for days.

Every few years an oil tanker accident causes a polluting oil slick. But even more oil drips into the sea from broken pipes and leaky taps.

ENERGY POLLUTION

Pollution is also caused by forms of energy, such as heat, light, sound, and radiation or radioactivity. These cause problems in the environment—and not only for people. For example, noisy boats on waterways mean that rare river dolphins cannot find food using their "sonar" or sound echoes.

Noise pollution comes from vehicles, trains, planes, and machines. It makes people feel tense, stressed, worried, and ill.

PLUNDERING EARTH

Shops and stores are filled with an endless range of goods and products. But such choice and convenience has a terrible price —a plundered, polluted planet.

STARTING MATERIALS

Industry and manufacturing need raw materials, such as rocks called ores which contain metals, and minerals like sulphur. Mining or quarrying these materials creates pollution.

Quarries and mines (left) leave ugly scars on the land. The rock minerals, formerly deep in the ground but now exposed, are washed away by rain, polluting nearby rivers.

The pollution caused by obtaining natural resources is greatly reduced by recycling (above)—especially glass, metals, paper, cardboard, and some types of plastics.

MASS PRODUCTION

Earth's raw materials and resources are changed greatly by manufacturing. They are processed into all kinds of plastics, metals, chemicals, and other materials, which do not exist in nature. These materials are processed into a vast array of items by industrial production lines. Usually, the items are used for a time, then thrown away. The plastics, chemicals, and other unnatural substances in them collect and cause environmental problems. Industry also uses huge amounts of energy from sources such as coal and oil, and these too cause many forms of pollution.

Modern "intensive" farming yields vast choices of foods and produce. But it also brings greater energy use and rural pollution.

Being GREEN

Some natural resources are renewable and cause little pollution. After a forest is cut for timber, it is planted with young trees for the future. Wood is a natural material, and after it's used, it rots back into the soil, avoiding problems of waste disposal.

As technology and manufacturing advance, factories become out of date and useless—dangerous, decaying hulks of pollution.

Sustainable timber use means planting new trees.

9

AIR SCARE

One of the most visible and harmful forms of pollution is dirty air. We cannot see through the dust, smog, and particles it contains, and we breathe its poisonous chemicals into our delicate airways and lungs.

PARTICULATE POLLUTION

Some pollutants in air are too small to see. Larger particles float and blow around like smoky dust. They blot out the view, clog air filters and machines, and get into our bodies to cause serious illness. Old diesel engines produce much of this particulate pollution.

Photochemical smog forms when polluting chemicals, especially from vehicle exhaust, change in sunlight. They clump into bigger particles.

Ancient statues (above) are being eaten away by the damaging, corrosive chemicals in urban air. In big cities such as Bangkok, Thailand, outdoor workers, like traffic police, wear masks to protect their lungs.

Hot topic

Air pollution is usually worse in crowded areas during warm, sunny, calm weather. City-dwellers suffer a great range of illnesses such as colds, coughs, wheezing and asthma, and lung infections, like bronchitis and pneumonia.

Hills around Mexico City trap its polluted air.

Cyclists in some cities wear masks to filter the air they breathe and to protect their eyes.

FAR AND WIDE

Air pollution is a special problem because it does not stay in one place. Winds and weather carry it huge distances, so that people far away suffer its harmful effects.

CATS TO THE RESCUE

CATS, catalytic converters, are now standard in new vehicle exhausts. They prevent some pollutants escaping into the air by using special metals such as palladium to speed up, or catalyze, chemical reactions. Hydrocarbons (HCs) and deadly carbon monoxide (CO) are changed by oxygen (O_2) in the air into water (H_2O) and less harmful, but still polluting, carbon dioxide (CO_2).

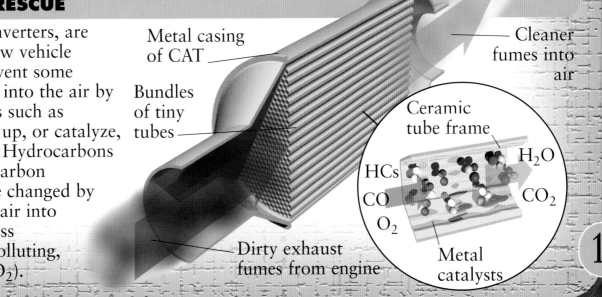

Metal casing of CAT

Bundles of tiny tubes

Cleaner fumes into air

Ceramic tube frame

HCs
CO
O_2

H_2O
CO_2

Dirty exhaust fumes from engine

Metal catalysts

Two particular kinds of air pollution are acid rain and ozone depletion. Steps have been taken to limit their damage in developed regions, especially the West, but developing nations still have much to do.

RAINING ACIDS

Smoke and fumes often contain a mixture of chemicals, including oxides of sulphur and nitrogen. They float into the air and dissolve in the tiny droplets of water which make up clouds, forming chemicals which are acidic and harmful. The cloud droplets eventually merge and fall as raindrops. The acids in the rain soak into soil and streams and damage trees and water life, such as fish.

Devices such as filters and scrubbers are now attached to many chimneys and smoke-stacks to capture or trap some of the acid-forming chemicals.

BATHED IN ACID

The main causes of acid rain are the smoke and fumes from power stations, factory chimneys, and vehicle exhaust. In the moisture and droplets of clouds, they form a mix of different acids.

Acid-forming chemicals in fumes

Trees suffer greatly from acid rain. Chemicals in the raindrops "burn" their leaves and make their roots incapable of taking up nutrients.

The polluted clouds can blow great distances on the wind before they release their moisture as acid rain. So the damage may happen far away from the original polluters, in remote wilderness areas.

Wind

Acid rain

CFCs in fridge cooling fluids need careful disposal.

CULPRIT CFCs

Ozone is a form of oxygen spread thinly in the air. It helps to protect the Earth from the Sun's more harmful rays, especially UV (ultraviolet) radiation. CFC (chlorofluorocarbon) chemicals get into the air from some types of aerosols and industrial processes. They destroy ozone, reducing its protective effect. This puts living things at risk for diseases such as cancer.

2002

2006

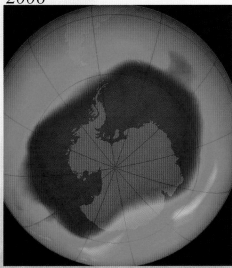

Being GREEN

Most aerosol sprays are now CFC-free, as shown by their labels. But they still contain many different chemicals. Making the spray cans also uses up natural resources. Pump-type sprays usually cause less harm to the environment.

Help the world: be CFC-free.

The way the world's winds and climate work means that ozone loss is greatest over the South Pole. Computer images show how the ozone "hole," where damage is worst (red-blue), varies from year to year.

13

Plants that grow in soil (dirt or earth) are the main foods of people around the world. Animals such as cattle and sheep eat plants too, and people eat their meat. So polluted soils affect our foods, us, and, of course, wildlife.

THE "-ICIDES"

Insecticides, herbicides, and fungicides are chemicals sprayed on farm plants or watered into their soil. The aim is to make the plants grow faster and better. However ...

Soil is so important to growing food and to the natural world. Scientists collect samples (right) and analyze them for polluting chemicals (below).

Some soil is so polluted that it is removed as a hazard to human life (below). But where is it dumped?

LASTING PROBLEMS

... Some of these chemicals can last for years. They kill small creatures such as caterpillars, worms, and mites, who normally help to keep the soil healthy. Certain chemicals are taken up by plants into their stems, leaves, and flowers. Animals eat the plants, and the chemicals collect in their bodies too. At any stage the pollution can cause harm. Sometimes this is not obvious for many years, until the damage is widespread.

In India, tea bushes (above) are sprayed to kill pests. But the workers lack protection and may be at risk.

Protesters warn of GM dangers.

Hot topic

Genetic Modification (GM) aims to improve farm crops and animals. But some nations, especially in Europe, have banned raising GM plants or livestock or selling their products.

GB01-99
*E321

GM crops are tested in fields.

15

Water is vital for life and an incredibly precious resource. It is an excellent solvent—substances dissolve or spread through it—and it is always on the move. It falls as rain, flows in streams and rivers to the sea, and soaks into soil. However, it can create problems.

Some water pollution is obvious, like acid in a French stream and debris at an Estonian power station. But much is unseen and invisible.

THE PROBLEM IS THE SOLUTION

Water dissolves all kinds of chemicals and pollutants, and then spreads them far and wide. The pollutants in this solution may affect aquatic life such as fish and waterbirds, who die from their toxic effects.

SOURCES OF WATER POLLUTION

Some rivers are like flowing garbage trucks that carry away wastes, chemicals, and other pollutants. But these substances do not disappear. They harm river life downstream. They collect in lakes and reach even more dangerous levels. The water can also be taken for irrigation, spreading the pollution to our fields and farms.

Farming
Pesticides, herbicides, and other chemicals are washed by rain into rivers.

Industry
Wastes and sewage pour from discharge pipes.

People
Water flows down drains and toilets, into the treatment and disposal system.

Downstream
Pollutants spread their damage far and wide.

Seepage
Water from far below brings up natural, but toxic, minerals.

Earthworks
Excavations, mines, and quarries loosen rocks and soil.

Hot topic
The Ganges of India is one of the world's largest, most sacred, and badly polluted rivers. Millions of people wash, bathe, collect water, and dispose of waste here. Anti-pollution and clean-up campaigns have been discussed, but with little progress.

Bathing in the Ganges: a religious ritual.

ACCIDENTALLY ON PURPOSE

Some chemicals get into the water by accident, from broken pipes or mistakenly opened taps at factories. But huge amounts of pollutants are dumped on purpose into rivers, lakes, and oceans, in the hope that they will spread out and dissipate. Some of them, however, will last for hundreds of years.

Too much of a good thing— fertilizers washed into rivers and oceans become food for tiny life-forms that cause a poisonous "red tide."

Oil polluted waters around San Francisco, California, in 2007 and Lake Charles, Louisiana, in 2006 (inset).

Radioactivity (radiation) is a form of energy given off by certain chemical substances, from their tiniest parts—atoms. It is invisible, but it can be deadly. Some types of radioactivity will last for thousands of years.

SOURCES OF RADIOACTIVITY

The main sources of radioactivity are the nuclear industry, especially nuclear or atomic power stations, and the weapons industry that makes nuclear missiles and atomic bombs. Small amounts are also used in medicine and scientific research.

TYPES OF RADIATION

Various natural substances emit radioactivity, but in very small amounts. It becomes much stronger when radioactive elements such as uranium and plutonium are purified and processed for nuclear power stations and weapons. They give off three forms of energy. Alpha and beta particles are parts of atoms, while gamma radiation is wave-like rays.

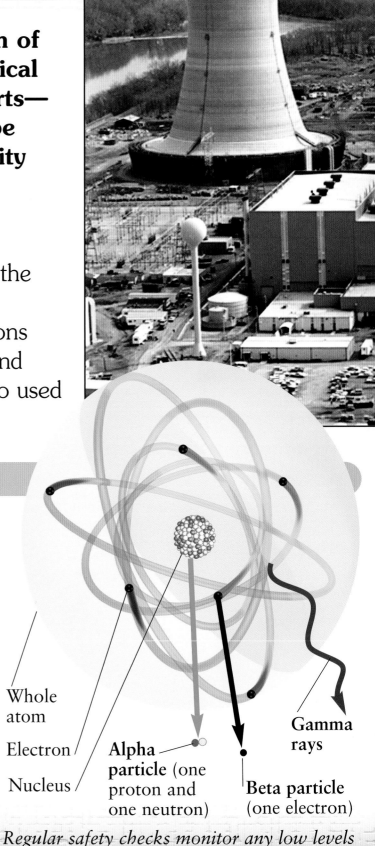

Whole atom

Electron

Nucleus

Alpha particle (one proton and one neutron)

Gamma rays

Beta particle (one electron)

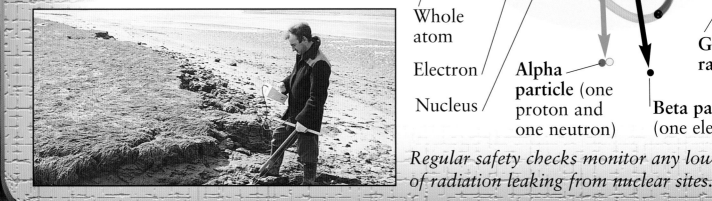

Regular safety checks monitor any low levels of radiation leaking from nuclear sites.

In 1979, the Three Mile Island Generating Plant, near Harrisburg, Pennsylvania, had a partial "meltdown" in its nuclear reactors (the two dome-topped buildings at center). Nuclear safety continues to generate huge debate.

Nuclear waste accumulates daily around the world. There is no safe, long-term way of disposing of it, so for now, it is simply stored.

DANGERS OF RADIATION

Radiation can cause sickness, skin sores, burns, tumors, cancers, and many other forms of illness—not only to people, but to animals, and damage to plant life. Most nuclear sites take great care that radiation does not escape. But there have been several accidents over the years. In 1986, at Chernobyl in the Ukraine, a power station exploded and polluted vast areas with radioactive dust. Hundreds of people died as a result. Lower levels of radioactivity can also leak into air and water and build up in the soil.

Being GREEN

World leaders meet regularly to discuss nuclear issues. Apart from radioactive pollution, there is a risk that terrorists might obtain nuclear material to make weapons such as "dirty bombs," which explode and spread deadly radiation over huge areas.

Presidents Vladimir Putin of Russia (left) and George Bush of the U.S. meet in 2007.

People often say: "Something should be done about pollution." We may say it ourselves. But really pollution is everyone's problem, and we can all do something about it. We can start in our daily lives, in our homes, schools, offices, and factories.

HOUSEHOLD CHEMICALS

Everything we pour down the sink or toilet goes into the water-treatment and sewage systems. Powerful chemicals such as bleach and strong cleansers force these systems to work harder.

ECOLOGICAL
LAUNDRY BLEACH
ECOVER
KEEPS WHITES BRIGHT
NATURALLY
CHLORINE FREE

HOW HOMES HELP

The modern kitchen's labor-saving gadgets are convenient—but they often waste energy and resources. It also costs money and energy to bring clean water in, and to take it away for treatment after use.

Friendly help
Some detergents, soaps, and cleaners are friendlier to the environment.

The contents of the garbage can must go somewhere—often into landfills, which may only store pollution for the future.

Too-hot spot Wasted heat means wasted energy.

Recycling
Suitable containers in handy places make recycling less of a chore.

Most stores stock environmentally-friendly products. They are made using fewer natural resources, more recycled materials, and less energy. In this way, they also reduce pollution and cleanup costs.

Hot topic

Public transportation can be quick, safe, and less environmentally harmful. But when underfunded, it is crowded, dirty, and unreliable. Pressure on politicians and officials can bring change, as it did with the Red Line in Chicago, Illinois.

Red Line carries 210,000 people daily.

Electric economy
Electrical devices left on can waste electricity, which means more pollution at the power station.

Drain strain
Dripping taps waste valuable water supplies and require more water disposal and treatment.

Time savers
Timers turn appliances on only when they are needed, saving money and energy.

Solar cells trap "free" light energy to charge batteries in electric vehicles, reducing pollution.

California has been testing Zero Emission buses and taxis since 2005.

OUT AND ABOUT

A person traveling by public transportation, such as the bus or train, causes up to 100 times less pollution than a person driving alone in a car. Many cities are developing electric trains, streetcars, and monorails, which do not pump harmful exhaust gases into the air and also reduce noise pollution.

Factories and industries make products that people buy. They also make profits so that they stay in business and provide jobs. But it is often difficult to be successful in industry while also avoiding pollution.

Iron, steel, and electronics industries are huge users of resources, so recycling their products is very important.

THE MAIN AIM

Industry and mass production help us by making consumer goods for our convenience. They can also help us by finding new ways of reducing harm to the environment. Many countries now have anti-pollution regulations, but sometimes industries find sneaky ways around these.

Leaders discuss global issues, like pollution. By 2008, the U.S. was the only major industrialized nation that had not signed the Kyoto climate change agreement.

Being GREEN

In the 1970s-'80s, concerns grew about the lead content in vehicle fuels such as gas. Lead made engines run more smoothly, but it also got into exhaust fumes and, if breathed in, possibly damaged the body's brain and nervous system. Most countries now have unleaded gas—but this still releases dangerous substances into the air.

Unleaded gas: better than leaded, but still polluting.

"POLLUTER PAYS"

As people become more aware of pollution dangers, laws and guidelines are changing. Formerly, it was necessary to prove that a polluting substance released by industry actually caused harm. More and more, it is now necessary for industry to prove that the substance does not cause harm, and also to pay for clean-ups or problems that result.

Filters or "scrubbers" on industrial smokestacks now remove most harmful fumes and chemicals, but not greenhouse gases.

23

The world now has more than 6.6 billion people, and this number rises faster every year. Most people want food, water, a place to live, and consumer goods such as cars and televisions, so the demand for these products is skyrocketing. Is there a limit to what our world can provide?

POPULATION PRESSURE

Populations rise fastest in Asia, Africa, and South America—where millions already struggle with hunger, poverty, disease, and polluted air, water, and soil. Also, since 2007, more people around the world live in cities and towns, rather than villages and the countryside. This forces more pollution into smaller areas.

Millions of People

- Sao Paulo, Brazil
- Buenos Aires, Brazil
- Mexico City, Mexico
- New York, New York
- Istanbul, Turkey
- Mumbai, India
- Karachi, Pakistan
- Moscow, Russian Fed.
- Delhi, India
- Dhaka, Bangladesh
- Jakarta, Indonesia
- Manila, Philippines
- Shanghai, China
- Seoul, South Korea
- Tokyo, Japan

HALTE! PLUS DE TIR AU BUT SANS CAPOTE!

Sida

HOTEL CONDOM

Some countries advise their citizens to have fewer children.

North America
490 million

Europe
800 million

South America
423 million

Africa
950 million

Asia
3.78 billion

Australia and Oceania
34 million

About 5 percent of the world's people own 95 percent of the world's wealth. This imbalance forces millions to survive in shanties, slums, and favelas, as seen here in Rio de Janeiro, Brazil.

CROWDED CITIES

Pollution problems are usually worse in cities where many people live close together and crowd into offices and factories. Even disposing of their bodily waste is a huge challenge, so that sewage does not foul the air, pollute water, and spread germs and disease.

Modern sewage works, such as this one in London, England, treat the human waste of thousands of people, while causing minimal pollution.

Being GREEN

Many cities encourage people to ride bikes rather than drive cars, by providing bike lanes that are safe and follow direct, useful routes. This saves money, reduces pollution, and is healthy exercise.

A cyclist in Milwaukee, Wisconsin

RICH AND POOR

The population in many rich countries is rising slowly, if at all. This means there is money not only for a comfortable lifestyle, but also to combat pollution. People in poorer areas see the lifestyle of the wealthy, and naturally, they want it too. But they have less money to spend, especially on caring for the environment, so pollution spirals out of control.

WILDLIFE IN TROUBLE

Winds and water currents carry pollution around the globe, even to remote mountaintops and polar regions. Some of the pollutants greatly harm wildlife.

UNSEEN DANGER

Many types of chemical pollutants have found their way to wilderness areas, where they damage plants and animals. A particular hazard known as bioaccumulation is shown below.

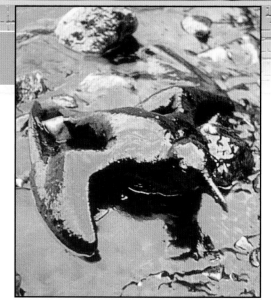

Birds try to clean oil from their feathers using their beaks, but they swallow oil in the process and soon die.

POLLUTANTS IN THE FOOD CHAIN

Levels of a pollutant may be so low in water that it is hardly noticed. But the chemical is taken in by plants, which are eaten by animals, who are in turn eaten, and so on along the food chain. At each stage the pollutant's level rises as it collects or accumulates in the body, then passes on. The animals at the end of the food chain accumulate high enough levels of the pollutant to suffer harm.

1 Polluting chemicals are very spread out or diluted in sea water.

2 Plankton (tiny plants and animals) take in small amounts.

3 Small fish eat plankton and absorb more of the pollutants.

4 Seals eat many fish, accumulating even more.

5 Pollutants are higher still in polar bears who eat fish and seals.

Hot topic
In 1988, thousands of seals died in the North Sea from a similar virus that causes distemper in dogs. Perhaps water pollutants reduced their resistance to infection. The problem returned in 2002 and killed half the seals in some areas.

A few sick seals recovered.

PROBLEM CHEMICALS

Examples of polluting chemicals include PCBs (polychlorinated biphenyls) used in industry and the organochlorides found in some pesticides and herbicides. These are not quickly biodegraded—they do not break down easily even after turning them into less harmful substances.

Pollution's effects may take years to show. The now-banned pesticide DDT collected in birds like peregrine falcons and affected their eggs, so they could not breed.

Field trials of pesticides and herbicides are carried out to check how much gets into the soil and for how long.

MANY EFFECTS

Some pollutant chemicals have direct effects, causing sores on an animal's body or eyes. Others get into the body and weaken the animal's resistance, so it can no longer fight off germs, diseases, and infesting parasites.

27

Some of the most dangerous effects of pollution are on our own bodies and minds. Chemicals in air, water, foods, and drinks may get into the body and cause damage—sometimes permanent.

TICKING TIME BOMB

Some effects of pollution on health are clear, such as chemicals that cause sickness and diarrhea. Other pollutants may cause only a few minor problems at first, like dizziness or weakness. In time, the pollutants accumulate to high levels and can lead to serious problems.

People who live near busy roadways may suffer more breathing problems than average. They are tested using a peak-flow meter.

In poor and crowded regions, the effects of pollution may be difficult to distinguish from other health hazards, such as lack of food, and water contaminated with germs.

A new well aims to bring clean water to an area. But some wells are polluted by natural substances like arsenic, which seep up from deep underground.

NATURE LENDS A HAND

There is much research into ways of absorbing polluting chemicals from the environment naturally, using living things —especially simple plants like algae, microbes such as bacteria, and fungi like mushrooms. Some of these are being genetically modified to take in large amounts of the pollutant from their surroundings, without suffering harm. Then these living things can be collected and disposed of in a safe way.

Lichens (combinations of algae and fungi) take in certain pollutants from the air, like "living sponges."

POLLUTION AND THE BODY

Almost every part of the body is at risk from some kind of pollution. Airways and lungs are vulnerable to airborne fumes and particles, and the digestive system to chemicals in foods and drinks. Damage to the brain and nerves tends to happen more slowly.

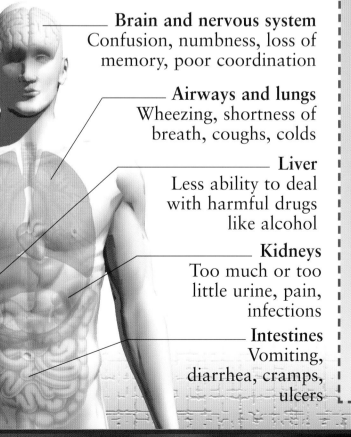

Brain and nervous system
Confusion, numbness, loss of memory, poor coordination

Airways and lungs
Wheezing, shortness of breath, coughs, colds

Liver
Less ability to deal with harmful drugs like alcohol

Kidneys
Too much or too little urine, pain, infections

Intestines
Vomiting, diarrhea, cramps, ulcers

Hot topic

In the 1950s, people near Minimata Bay, Japan, suffered many health problems. The cause was toxic mercury used by local industry, emptied into the bay and taken up by shellfish and fish, which people then ate. Other toxic chemical tragedies include Bhopal, India, in 1984, Abidjan, Ivory Coast, in 2006, and Kipevu, Kenya, in 2008.

Minimata memorial, Japan

It's easy to blame pollution on everyone else. Yet we can all take action to reduce the problem and make our world safer and cleaner.

STEPS TO TAKE

Everyday around the home, at school and work, while shopping, traveling, and spending our free time—we can be aware of pollution. There are many ways to tackle the problem: waste less, recycle more, conserve natural resources, choose environmentally-friendly products, support groups that identify polluters, and campaign for a cleaner, greener future in our world.

FOR MORE INFORMATION

Organizations

ENVIRONMENTAL PROTECTION AGENCY (EPA)
EPA Headquarters
Ariel Rios Building
1200 Pennsylvania Avenue, NW
Washington, DC 20460
www.epa.gov/
The agency of the federal government of the United States charged with protecting human health and with safeguarding the natural environment including air, water, and land.

FRIENDS OF THE EARTH
1717 Massachusetts Avenue,
Suite 600
Washington, DC 20036
(202) 783-7400
www.foe.org/
The largest international network of environmental groups in the world, represented in more than 70 countries, campaigning for a safer, greener future, including reducing all kinds of pollution.

THE NATURE CONSERVANCY
4245 North Fairfax Drive,
Suite 100
Arlington, VA 22203-1606
(703) 841-5300
www.nature.org
The leading conservation organization working around the world to protect ecologically important lands and waters for nature and people.

ORGANIC CONSUMERS ASSOCIATION
6771 South Silver Hill Drive
Finland, MN 55603
(218) 226-4164
www.organicconsumers.org/
The leading lobbying organization for organic food and farming in the U.S., campaigning on issues.

PLANET ARK
www.planetark.com/
Not-for-profit, Internet-based organization that shows how we can all reduce our day-to-day impact on the environment.

For further reading

Desonie, Dana. *Atmosphere: Air Pollution and Its Effects* (Our Fragile Planet). New York, NY: Chelsea House Publications, 2007.

Jefferis, David. *Green Power: Eco-Energy without Pollution* (Science Frontiers). New York, NY: Crabtree Publishing, 2006.

Kidd, J.S. and Renee. *Air Pollution: Problems and Solutions* (Science and Society). New York, NY: Facts on File, 2005.

Miller, Debra A. *Pollution* (Current Controversies). Farmington Hills, MI: Greenhaven Press, 2007.

Orme, Helen. *Pollution* (Earth in Danger). New York, NY: Bearport Publishing, 2008.

Spilsbury, Louise. *Environment at Risk: The Effects of Pollution* (Geography Focus). Chicago, IL: Raintree, 2006.

Web Sites

Due to the changing nature of Internet links, Rosen Publishing has developed an online list of Web sites related to the subject of this book. This site is updated regularly. Please use this link to access the list: http://www.rosenlinks.com/pic/poll

GLOSSARY

CAT
Catalytic convertor, a device that removes some harmful substances and pollutants from the exhaust fumes of cars and other vehicles.

CFCs
Chlorofluorocarbons, industrial chemicals which have an especially damaging effect on the ozone in the atmosphere.

environment
The surroundings, including soil, rocks, water, air, plants, animals, and even human-made structures.

ore
Rocks or similar substances from the Earth which contain useful amounts of minerals or metals, such as iron, aluminum, or sulphur.

ozone
A form of the gas oxygen, which is spread through the atmosphere and helps to protect the Earth's surface against some of the Sun's damaging ultraviolet rays.

PCBs
Polychlorinated biphenyls, chemicals from industry that can harm living things.

pesticide
A substance designed to kill or disable pests such as insects or worms, especially on farm crops or animals.

pollutant
A substance that causes damage to the environment, including to wildlife and humans.

recycle
To use something again, or to take it apart or break it up and use the substances it was made from again.

smog
A combination of fumes, particles, and gases, especially from vehicle exhausts, that causes a harmful haze in the air.

toxic
Harmful, poisonous, or damaging.